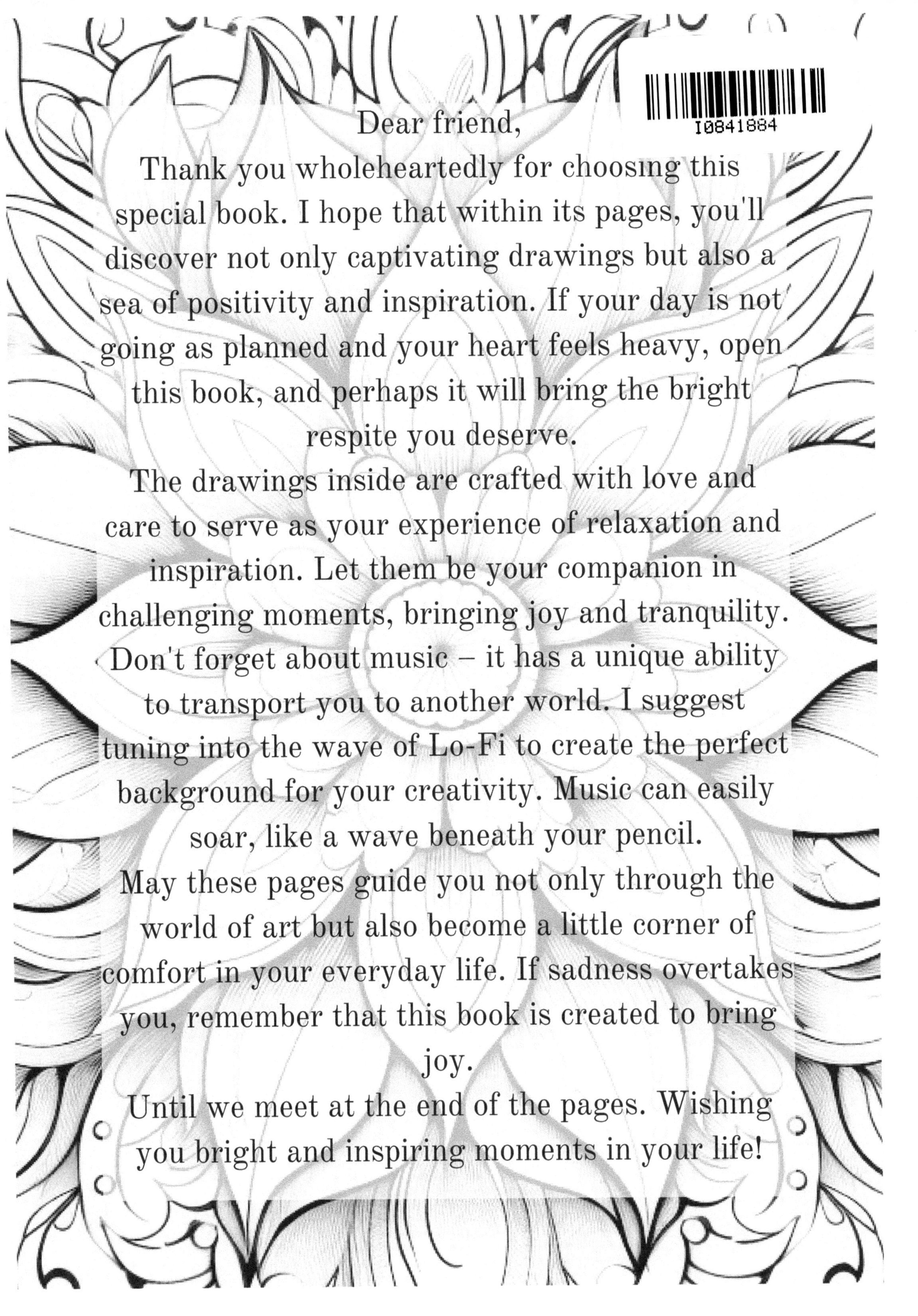

Dear friend,

Thank you wholeheartedly for choosing this special book. I hope that within its pages, you'll discover not only captivating drawings but also a sea of positivity and inspiration. If your day is not going as planned and your heart feels heavy, open this book, and perhaps it will bring the bright respite you deserve.

The drawings inside are crafted with love and care to serve as your experience of relaxation and inspiration. Let them be your companion in challenging moments, bringing joy and tranquility. Don't forget about music – it has a unique ability to transport you to another world. I suggest tuning into the wave of Lo-Fi to create the perfect background for your creativity. Music can easily soar, like a wave beneath your pencil.

May these pages guide you not only through the world of art but also become a little corner of comfort in your everyday life. If sadness overtakes you, remember that this book is created to bring joy.

Until we meet at the end of the pages. Wishing you bright and inspiring moments in your life!

Hello again! Meeting you at the end of this wonderful book fills me with joy. I hope it brought warmth and vibrant colors to your day, and now a smile is lighting up your face.

Allow me to share a bit about the incredible journey we've undertaken together, spending over 137 hours – the time it takes to infuse every page of this book with colors and inspiration. This path is not just a collection of drawings; it's a story of our encounters, discoveries, and personal creativity.

During this time, you haven't just filled pages with color; you may have discovered new facets within yourself. Perhaps, creativity has become not just a moment of drawing but an exploration of your inner strength, a source of inspiration in other aspects of life. Maybe these hours of drawing have been a time for self-discovery and a deep dive into your inner world.

On the next page, I've shared thoughts on the changes you may have noticed in yourself over more than 100 hours of drawing. I hope they serve as a familiar sign of vibrant creative growth for you.

This book is more than just tasks; it reflects your inner world. Allow yourself to fully grasp these transformations that have occurred within you, and may the smile on your face be a bright testament to our creative journey together.

How will 100 hour drawing bring about changes?
Stress and Anxiety Management
One of the primary effects of drawing is the ability to effectively manage stress and anxiety. Daily practice will help you learn to control your emotions, release accumulated tension, and find inner peace in any situation.
Improvement in Concentration and Productivity
Regular drawing contributes to improved concentration and mental clarity. You will notice how your ability to focus on tasks becomes better, ultimately enhancing your productivity and efficiency in both work and daily activities.
Enhancement of Mental Well-being
Drawing contributes to strengthening mental well-being. It can help you perceive the world around you more harmoniously, improve self-esteem, and cultivate a positive attitude toward life.
Better Quality of Sleep
Drawing has a positive impact on the quality of sleep. The practice helps you relax and calm your mind before bedtime, promoting a deeper and more restorative rest.
Physical Health
Drawing is associated with an overall improvement in physical health. It can help reduce blood pressure, stress levels, and inflammation in the body. Deep breathing during drawing contributes to these positive effects.
Increase in Self-awareness and Spiritual Growth
Daily drawing fosters the development of self-awareness and spiritual growth. You will gain a better understanding of yourself, your needs, and values, as well as acquire a deeper understanding of your life and the world.